Getting to School

Around the World

by Dan Adams

People in different places get to school in different ways.

Some areas have many roads. Children in these areas often go to school by car, like these students in Mexico.

Mexico

Another way children in these areas can get to school is by bus, like these students in the United States.

United States

Many people live in places surrounded by water. In these areas, children don't get to school by car. They get there by boat, like these children in Malaysia.

Malaysia

Some areas flood when there is a lot of rain. How do children in these areas get to school? Like these children in Botswana, they get there by boat.

Botswana

In some areas, there may not be many good roads. Some families do not have cars, and there may not be many buses. Many children in these areas go to school on foot, like these children in the countryside of India.

India

In some areas, children may walk an hour or more to get to school, like these children in Kenya.

Kenya

Some cities and towns have very crowded roads, but this doesn't stop children from getting to school. In Tokyo, the capital of Japan, the streets are very crowded, but students can get to school easily by subway.

Japan

In parts of Vietnam, many students get to school by bicycle and by scooter.

Vietnam

Some places are very snowy. It can be difficult to travel by car or by bus on snowy roads. Many Inuit children in Canada ride snowmobiles to school.

Canada

Children get to school in different ways
all around the world.
How do YOU get to school?

Mongolia

Facts About Transportation

The ways people travel have changed through time. A long time ago, people only traveled on animals like horses or camels, but in the late 1800s and 1900s, many new types of transportation were invented. This timeline shows a few of them.

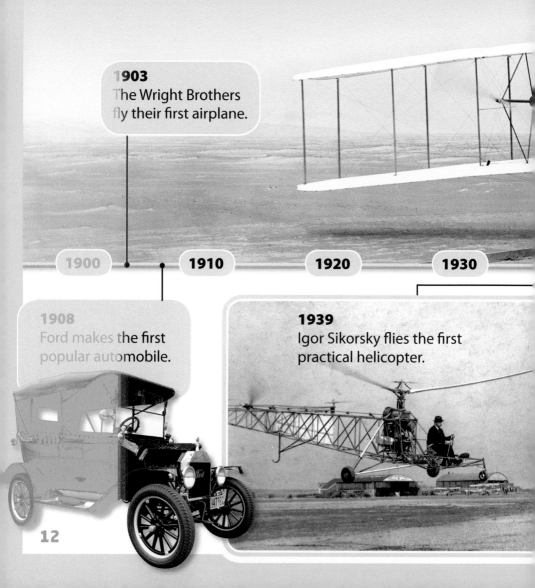

1903
The Wright Brothers fly their first airplane.

1900   1910   1920   1930

1908
Ford makes the first popular automobile.

1939
Igor Sikorsky flies the first practical helicopter.

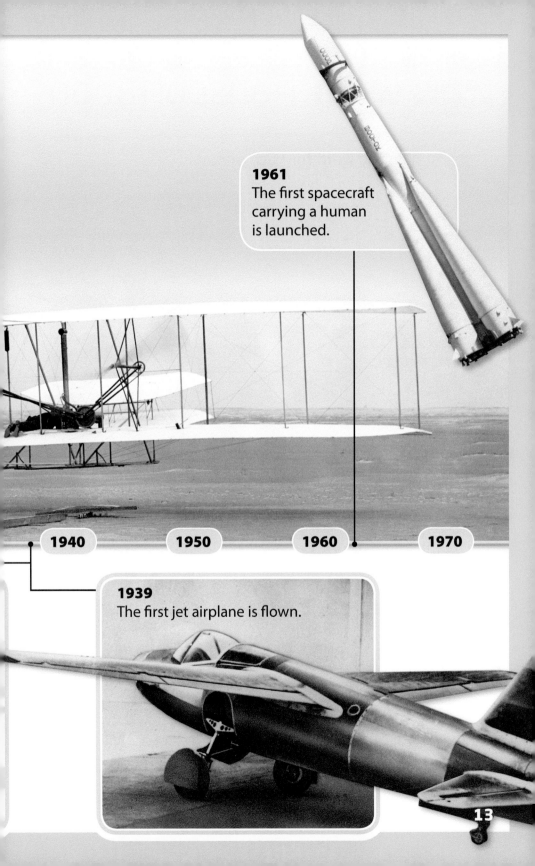

1961
The first spacecraft carrying a human is launched.

1940　　　1950　　　1960　　　1970

1939
The first jet airplane is flown.

13

Fun with Transportation

Unscramble the word for each picture.

> boat   car   scooter   subway

r c a

1. ___car___

t a b o

2. _____

b u w y a s

3. _____

o r t s o c e

4. _____

How are the people traveling? Write the answer.

| by scooter | by bicycle | by subway | on foot |

1. ___by scooter___   2. _____

3. _____   4. _____

How fast is each way of traveling?
Write them in order from slowest to fastest.

___on foot___ _____ _____ _____

slowest   **fastest**

Glossary

capital the most important city or town of a country

cities large places where many people live

crowded many people or things in one place

flood to cover dry land with water

roads streets on which cars, buses, and trucks drive

surrounded to have something on all sides